Wu Wei

ALSO BY TOM CRAWFORD

The Temple on Monday
China Dancing
Lauds
If It Weren't For Trees
I Want To Say Listen

Wu Wei

Tom Crawford

MILKWEED EDITIONS

Published 2006 by Milkweed Editions
Printed in Canada
Cover design by Kyle G. Hunter
Cover art: sketch adapted from traditional acupuncture diagram;
        bird images courtesy istockphoto.com
Author photo by Michael Selker
Interior design by Rachel Holscher
Interior illustrations courtesy istockphoto.com
The text of this book is set in 10.5/15 Minion Pro.
06 07 08 09 10   5 4 3 2 1
First Edition

Milkweed Editions, a nonprofit publisher, gratefully acknowledges sustaining support from
Emilie and Henry Buchwald; Bush Foundation; Patrick and Aimee Butler Family Foundation;
Cargill Value Investment; Timothy and Tara Clark Family Charitable Fund; Dougherty Family
Foundation; Ecolab Foundation; General Mills Foundation; Greystone Foundation; Institute
for Scholarship in the Liberal Arts, College of Arts and Sciences, University of Notre Dame;
Constance B. Kunin; Marshall Field's Gives; McKnight Foundation; a grant from the
Minnesota State Arts Board, through an appropriation by the Minnesota State Legislature,
a grant from the National Endowment for the Arts, and private funders; an award from
the National Endowment for the Arts, which believes that a great nation deserves great art;
Navarre Corporation; Debbie Reynolds; St. Paul Travelers Foundation; Ellen and Sheldon
Sturgis; Target Foundation; Gertrude Sexton Thompson Charitable Trust (George R. A.
Johnson, Trustee); James R. Thorpe Foundation; Toro Foundation; Serene and Christopher
Warren; W. M. Foundation; and Xcel Energy Foundation.

Library of Congress Cataloging-in-Publication Data

Crawford, Tom, 1939–
    Wu wei / Tom Crawford.— 1st ed.
        p. cm.
    ISBN-13: 978-1-57131-423-9 (pbk. : acid-free paper)
    ISBN-10: 1-57131-423-7 (pbk. : acid-free paper)
    I. Title.

    PS3553.R296W82 2006
    811'.54—dc22

                                                    2005031215

This book is printed on acid-free paper.

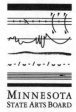

NATIONAL
ENDOWMENT
FOR THE ARTS
Established 1965

MINNESOTA
STATE ARTS BOARD

THIS BOOK IS DEDICATED TO MY FRIEND,

Len Hudson.

Wu Wei

II. Suggestions for Making a Temple

"We can do no great things—
only small things, with great love."

—MOTHER TERESA

Wu Wei

To let one's mind alone. This is *wu wei* since *wu* means not or non and *wei* means action—doing, straining, or busyness. In its Buddhist subtext, doing nothing is doing everything.

"Nothing is whole that has not been rent."

—RAINER MARIA RILKE

The Journey Out

CHENGDU

This morning
aren't we just a little bit famous
in the world, all of us,
putting our feet down
on the cold floor one more time,
trying it out—
Oh, and the world,
if it is turning to the right
then we, aren't we all leaning to the left,
our tee shirts, hats flying,
interchangeable
on this long train to Chengdu.

Riding soft-sleeper with a window seat,
I'm the resident poet—
my English curving into your Chinese
is simply love of the sounds
I'm trying so hard to make,
the rough roadbed
throwing us every which way,
the tea spilling over.

Einstein had a similar experience
and used the train, the whistle
blowing through the night,
to advance his own theory of poetry—
dark smoke
trailing back for miles, the voice
swelling out of a tunnel,
morning again, its heavy engine

pulling the curve
and first light we shape our words with.

"*Chengdu*," the conductor says,
tipping his blue hat,
"Chengdu, ten minutes."

ZAI JIAN

To just not move.
And all around me it's Chinese.
Autumn Festival, the heaviness of this old air
with its mooncakes and stares
banging me in the head every day.
I've stopped saying, "I'm really here."
And the chorus of morning spitters,
well, you get used to it.
Words, words arrive, the right ones
when you least expect them.
Yesterday I said to myself
for the first time, *zai jian. Good-bye.*
It's something I'm always rehearsing.
Next block over someone has died.
Firecrackers are driving away the bad spirits.
In the open market in Lieschimu
the peasants from the countryside
like to come up real close to my face.
They want to look at me,
they just want to look.

LAUNDRY

Up close the pile of white laundry
turns into a hundred geese
riding on top of the dirty bus ahead of us,
tied down like the Chinese luggage
and altogether calm about the journey
except for one or two
who look at the passing countryside
with raised heads.

WHAT'S PRETTY HERE

No angel holding up the wet chicken
just bled out.
Already old, she shows her small daughter
how the Chinese pluck feathers,
where the knife goes in
between the neck and the crop
big as a baseball
from all the stones
the chicken had to eat
its last day on earth,
and how to slide her child's small hand
into the cavity
and around the warm entrails
to pull out with them
the heart and trachea.

Play still diverts her, though,
the hot tub full of dead chickens
she stirs with a stick
humming something her mother taught her
in the countryside.

What's pretty here,
the tired father, head down in the sun,
over his work
and the light in the dirty water
the child bangs with her stick
pushing, now and then,
a dead chicken down.

It's been a few years since that howling autumn wind took off your thatched roof and scattered the straw in the limbs of the alders across the river, and just when you were getting settled in. Then it rained. I'm here now by your famous cottage and where you probably once stood. Everything is pretty much as you left it in your poems. Some things hang on. The river still flows. And the wind that pushed you around that morning took off my hat this afternoon. So what does that say about the so-called distance between us, the living and the dead? Your trees survive. After all, who can improve on bamboo or the grove you planted? A tiny breath of wind sets them off. A shy bird with yellow feet scratches among the dry leaves. This afternoon we toasted you in the local teahouse. It's the damnedest thing, say *"Dufu"* anywhere in China and everybody knows you. An old woman sitting at our table beams a toothy smile. Out of nowhere warm bowls of rice arrive and the family at our table insists on sharing their roast duck. What's beauty but longing? Brothers in this life, we write our poems.

CIQIKOU

China is toothless
and retired in Ciqikou.
A lot of old men
in faded blue jackets
with big black buttons
swell the teahouses
with their stories,
the good ones, made up
where the past always wins out
over what's ahead,
and all day long they smoke to it
while they swirl the boiling water
through the old leaves
green as bamboo.
Nothing new happens in Ciqikou.
The stone streets are narrow
and quiet
and all run downhill
to where the wide Jialing flows by.

CALL TO ME IN CHINA

Over the phone
from the other side of the world
my dear friend tells me
my old cat has died.

I can see Gati now, curled up,
asleep
in a box of marigolds
where I left her
in the warm sun in August
in America.

Dying is always choosing
between one pale star
and another—groping around
out there for the beloved.
It's the oldest poem alive—
what is given to us for the asking,
then taken.

HUNAN

Up ahead the water buffalo
can imagine hay
under his black nose
and his warm stall in yellow light.

What does he know about
how he looks from behind
or history
coming through the mud

It is all he can do every day
just to pull his great weight forward
ahead of the plow.

In his soft eyes a small boy
makes faces in the water,
sticks out his tongue,

and a hard wind from Hunan
carries a crow away.

STREETS

1.

Two street monkeys do back
flips, three, four times while a scruffy
blond dog, part of the act,
pretends it's chasing them
barking commands.
It's a real crowd pleaser.
When people begin clapping,
a Chinese midget in black
topcoat with tails
comes around
holding out a blue, felt hat.

2.

Both are blind. One plays the *erhu*
and the other sings. Most
of the Chinese gathered around
are themselves poor.
It's like tearing a book in half
to listen to them. This is not
the charming folk music
from the countryside they are playing.
No one wants to hear it,
but no one leaves.
Their marble eyes roll involuntarily,
telling us they were born like this.
Wherever they go in China
they have to grope their way.
Here for an hour in Shapingba
they are like the Sisters of Mercy.

They cannot even find us
on the sidewalk
but they draw a crowd,
they provide.

3.

The old woman arranges
her several dead rats
by size on the wooden table.
The larger ones in front,
all the heads pointing
toward the street, the long tails
curled over the fat bodies.
Then she waves her hand
over them, smiling.
It's only good marketing.
She's saying, "See for yourself,
my poison works."

4.

A man abruptly stops
on the sidewalk to clear his lungs
before he spits. He is a long time
at it. People walk around him.
Buses go by. A dog stops
momentarily to watch.
It is so deep, this gravelly note,
he can only bring it part way
up. It's a relief to see him

finally straighten up
and begin to walk,
adjusting his pants.

5.

It stops raining. In Jie fang bei a one-legged man in dirty
clothes hobbles out of an alley on a wooden crutch, spreads a
red, white, and blue plastic tarp on the muddy sidewalk and sits
down. Immediately, as if they were waiting for him, a crowd of
the curious form around him. From a clean stack of white paper
he slides off a sheet. He turns it over. Rubs a hand over each side.
Holds it up to the light. Decides. Then, with his large hand and
broken nails he pulls a wide calligrapher's brush across the sheet
in a single, confident stroke, laying down a wide, waving line
of black ink in the shape of a gnarled branch growing from the
trunk of a tree somewhere off the paper. Quickly, with a smaller
brush, he paints in shoots and blossoms. Now, for the first time
the audience stirs. One man hands the man next to him a ciga-
rette. And when, with a gentle twist of his hand, five, six times,
the artist adds two songbirds, one with its beak open, every-
body is pleased. They nudge each other, smile. Then an old man
with no teeth points to the sky, holding his palm open to show
us. Someone in the back hurriedly moves forward and over the
drawing opens a yellow umbrella.

6.

In Nanchong a mother turns
her three-year-old son around
on the sidewalk and points at me

walking by. "*Lao wai, lao wai*," she says.
His small eyes widen
in perceptible notches.
He already knows a duck is not a chicken
in China—that's easy—but this?
In order to think about it
he backs into his mother's legs,
pulls her red dress around him,
then looks up and down the street
to see if there are any more of us.

7.

Grotesque to look at,
the naked leg coming straight out
from his body, on display,
a gaping wound running almost
the length of it, that glistens red.
Sometimes bright rivets hold
the flesh together,
the leg swollen, the skin
stretched tight as a balloon.
Exactly the response he'd hoped for,
the one you probably have
on your face looking down at him
on the sidewalk.
Now you're both sad-eyed.
All the time he's rubbing it
he holds the other hand out to you,
palm open. But if the dreaded street
inspector should come, he's up

in a flash, grabbing his money
with one hand, his third leg
with the other, tucking it inside
his coat. It's a class act,
even the way he vanishes
into the crowd.

8.

I'm smiling. Mao, scaled up
to five times his actual size
and tied down with ropes,
is being backed up to the site
where the waiting crane
will carefully lower him into position
once it has been decided
which way he's supposed to point.
Krissy jabs me with her elbow,
"Don't laugh," she says. She's right.
By now a large crowd
of Chinese have gathered. Carved
from white marble, in this incarnation
he will cost the school plenty.
I'm thinking, Mao and my father,
they had a lot in common. Both
big men. Sons of farmers.
And both wanted order.
They knew just where the hoe
belonged or the shovel in the tool shed.
One day my father knocked me ass over
appetite—his expression—when I failed

to return a tool, I forget which one,
to the shed, to the exact place
assigned to it. I couldn't hear
out of my right ear for weeks
after that blow. And both men
felt stronger, too, pointing at the landscape—
what they wanted for the future,
where the house would be built.
My father, right until the end,
had a plan. Fathers and sons,
that's what's going on here,
isn't it—China, the obedient son,
Mao the malevolent father. China
has a look-alike Mao now, a movie
star (I saw him one day in front
of the Chongqing Hotel with news people)
a big orphan boy from the countryside.
Even the old generals tremble and pull
themselves to attention when he enters the room.

SHI BA TI

In summer the Yangtze flows swift,
deep. Is this where Mao swam across?
She doesn't know, the lady
carrying the hot kettle with the long spout.
But she can hit our cups from two feet away
and the two old men sharing our table
only insist that we smoke with them
while they tell us about the end of the Manchu
and cutting off their pigtails.

Here, Sichuan Opera, they argue,
the only mandate from heaven,
mimes old China from behind a torn blanket
where suddenly pots and pans bang
and the bleating *erhu* plays,
announcing the end of civilization
or the beginning with the fool stepping out.

Through clouds of cigarette smoke
his red tongue wriggles and darts
in time with his arching black eyebrows
and glittering rosy eyelids fluttering
like exotic birds, the plot everybody knows
by heart—stamp their feet too—vanity, despair.

Now we forget the dirt floor under us
when the heroine in blue silk glides
in tiny steps across the makeshift stage,
turning her head, by slow degrees, toward us.
Black fish embroidered on her six-foot-long sleeves
hang to the floor, symbolizing long life,
happiness.

No one in China can imagine a better life
than a long one. Another chance to recall the past.
The intensity of her eyes that never blink
could be this country, her hands
hidden under so much silk.

The tall magistrate smiles too much,
stroking with thumb and finger his official beard.
"No blame," the *I Ching* would say, in this world
we need him too.
So what's to witness?
The props falling over.
An ambush foiled.
The clash of rubber swords.

Two workers packing smoked pig faces into a cardboard box run into trouble. One face, it turns out, is so large one man can't fit it into the box with the other, smaller faces. He tries everything—putting the face in the box sideways, at an angle, upside down. He even removes the sharp bamboo stretcher from behind the face. Then, seeing the difficulty, his fellow worker comes around to help him. Together they can fold the huge, orange ears over all right, but the face itself, even with the splint removed, is too fat to fold and the nose too big to bend down. In frustration the worker yanks the face from the box, slips, and the pig flies up and slaps him, hard. The blow almost knocks him down. Now he is embarrassed and he has grease on the side of his face, which he won't touch. His fellow worker looks away. The pig face is lying there at his feet where he dropped it, looking up at him with that sneer pigs get when they've been smoked. Other people, too, have stopped to watch him fight the pig or the ghost of a pig or something none of us can quite put our finger on.

BIRD WALK

Old age and freedom
so long in coming
they can hardly stay awake for it,
these retired party members
who sometimes doze off
in the morning sun
down in Lieschimu,
their arms around their caged birds.

I look inside to see
what it is they love so much.
This brown-headed solitary bird
with green eyelids,
inimical to ruffled feathers, seems to know
its company, alone, is enough.
If it moves at all I can't tell.
By its gold-knuckled toes
it maintains center
on a single perch.

Moved by my interest,
the old men always smile to see me coming.
One points to the new door he's added—
a tiny bamboo grove etched in thin bronze.
He is especially happy
about the blue-green patina
I trace with my fingers.
Each has his own logo
written in Chinese over the entrance.
Blue Cloud Gate on one, Cold Mountain
on another.

What's standardized here?
That the men all be old.
That the cages look like cages
and the small doors, whatever their design,
open inward.

HAN

We have come here to be stalled
by our own green hearts,
waylaid by what's past,
the way in crosshatched
and slow as the oldest painting,
the black buffalo
small against the mountain
still pulls the whole country along
on a single plow,
one hoof at a time.

RAIN

Rain in Chongqing is pretty much
like rain in Portland—
it comes down wet from Heaven
and when it's sudden,
without warning,
in both cities people shriek
and scatter. Newspapers double
for umbrellas,
dirty sidewalks glisten,
a mother runs out
to pull in her little boy.
Flags go up everywhere
in excitement—"We surrender,
we surrender."

DHARMA

With the butt of his last one
the tired bus driver
lights a fresh cigarette,
sips some green tea
from his glass jar of old leaves,
and, as if to save the best for last,
spits out the window
into Lieschimu, where I live.
It's a kind of offering,
I think, to another day lived,
to the old song inside,
and to turning
the dirty bus around.

YUAN FEN

The worn bowl
we eat from is always home.
I took nothing from China
it didn't want from me.
So, here is my heart
where the Jialing River
joins the great Yangtze.
The world here,
broken and dirty,
feeds me, sings.

Return

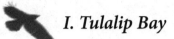 *I. Tulalip Bay*

WU WEI

Walk the same beach enough
and wigeon stay put,
gulls too. You become common
like bullwhip washed up
or broken soft-shell.
Driftwood becomes you
sitting for hours alone,
reciting the sutra of doing nothing.
What's more exciting than a wind shift,
a patch of green water close by,
its back suddenly up, a surprise riff
running against the tide.
You can't think your way to anything
around water this old.
The Talmud, Bible,
it doesn't matter, won't stack up
to the invisible column of air
eagles ride or water
lapping ordinary light. A beach,
after a while, just grinds you down
to quiet, where words—even the good ones,
the fuss they make—won't last.
Yes, yes, I'm here. Look at me.
Resolved. My broken walking stick
writing the names of those I love
in the sand.

WHATEVER I CAN MAKE OF THIS I HAVE

The brisk rubbing together of the hands,
my Asian apology for the innumerable lapses of love.
The heart's big ship too often moored.

The new day, nevertheless, coming in right on schedule.

The lighted world, a blue mote, a morning sweet
God rolls in His mouth.

A sprinkling of goldeneyes, feeding on kelp.

Failure, whatever I can make of you, I have.
You're like a new bride coming into the room.
Petals floating in a white dish.

Everything's forgiven.

PIGEON GUILLEMOT

February 20, and I would like to think
that I saw them first, coming ashore.
I don't mean walking but rather,
the way they do, first picking themselves up
out of the surf, altogether determined,
then aiming their small, black bodies at the holes
and crevices in the high cliffs,
half the time aborting the mission
halfway there or after discovering
another auk already inside.
Unable to hover
they only get one shot. Then back
to the water to consider
where they went wrong.
Think blood-red rhubarb
and you have the color of their feet
splayed out in front of them for the landing.
It's not beauty though but failure
I most connect with—like the feathered equivalent
of the little engine that could, back one goes,
a different hole this time, tumbling in.
You could call it play, the thing they have to do
and why shouldn't they, having come this far,
throw themselves into it?

and here's what I say:
God's not into sadness. He says it's a waste of time.
So, the grief I feel almost every day,
what Buddha says we've got coming to us,
should not be all that drives these—
what shall I call them?—earned poems.
I don't know if this proves it but I just came off the beach
with my dog, Walt. The whole way out and back
in a cool rain he ran from scent to luxurious scent,
poking his nose into washed-up seaweed,
rolling in what was left of a dead seagull, rotten fish,
pissing on those things worthy of it
and almost everything was.
I'm trying to learn from my little dog
that there is nothing that is not God, is not here
for our happiness. Me, all the time I'm sunk down
in my wet jacket, unforgiving of a botched love
while he pesters me with a soggy stick, tells me
to throw it, please throw it.

COMPANION TO A LOON

So you died, caught, I'll bet
in that gill net out there
held up by those big orange balls
stretched halfway across Tulalip Bay.
The Indian fisherman had to haul you up
then disentangle you
like so much stringy, green kelp.
It's unnatural that you should drown
that way, a perfect invention to water.
I'm sure I watched you the day before
yesterday, working the quiet shallows
around the boat dock
straight out from my little cabin.
Listen bird, I'm past making death sad.
The tide has no time for wakes
or tragedies. We're either coming in
or going out. It's like that,
the soul for a while boxed up
in feathers or this frail
human body of mine.
I'm just taking a little time out
from my walk because, well,
your drowned body is here
at my feet, even in death,
moving, unruffled.

With an Indian there is nothing you can do
or say to make him smile back. You're white
and that's that. If you need to be loved
you'd better go somewhere else.
Just another white man moved into Tulalip Bay.
Two chapters in local history is enough
to know why we're past noticing.
So, I hang back when the chum come in.
I know he knows I'm there watching him
let out the gill net from his small boat
as he motors across the quiet inland water
between the spit and the docks
along Mission Beach Road. The story goes,
in the 1920s, Snoqualamie Jim,
one of the elders who owned this finger of land,
got drunk and sold it all
to a Seattle businessman. No matter.
It's pretty much all white now
surrounded by water and Indian gill nets,
crab pots and something like a moral
certainty which is harder to put your finger on.
"How long have your people been here,"
I ask an Indian on the beach one day
knowing it's a dumb question,
but we were so close I wanted to say something.
He's silent for a long time, looking
mostly over my shoulder at the rock cliffs
behind us. "Oh," he says, "forever."
That's close enough I think
and for the distance that divides us.
His wave back going down the beach
is all right with me. I'll take what I can get.

I'M SIXTY-TWO

Another day ignorant.
Here comes the sun anyway.
So beautiful I could just pee my pants.
Frost wore diapers after seventy
his daughter told his biographer
he'd get so excited.
It doesn't get easier.
I just filleted a yellow perch
I caught an hour ago in the bay.
Its long gut unfolded
like origami,
one sand shrimp after another.
You see what I mean?
I live alone to spare myself,
another, the intensity of feelings
even a little bird brings on,
eating the bread crumbs
I put out the night before.

Stop for two Indians? Sure, why not. Brother and sister it turns out. "Thank ya honey," she says, sliding across the seat next to me. Hair bleached but the black showing through. Blue tattoos on both hands, not the professional kind. Look more like scrimshaw, tiny, blue fish on her thumbs. By the time he crowds into the little Toyota pickup behind her there's no room for Walt except right on top of them. "It's okay," the brother says, holding Walt in his big hands. "We like dogs." It's chilly. The windows are up. Our little cab suddenly fills with the smell of cigarettes and booze. What's he going to do, break Walt's neck, threaten to if I don't do what they say. Who's got the gun? Fuck, why'd I pick them up anyway? "My name's Joe and this is my sister," and his right hand reaches over her to shake mine. "Dogs really love ya, don't they," looking down at Walt, scratching his head. His sister's left hip is hard pressed into mine. It's not amusement, but something else on her face. "My last dog died," he says, bending his head around to look at me. "They don't live long like us, do they . . . knock on wood," and he taps the dashboard, all the time flashing this big, boyish smile. "Once I had a deep cut on my leg that didn't wanta heal. My uncle told me to let the dog lick it. Damn, if it didn't too after a few days of that." Walt likes the smell of them. He pushes his body into the sister's coat, into her neck. Her tattooed hand comes up to touch him, to rest on his back. "Where ya going?" I ask. "Ah, just up the road, Priest Point, either store it don't matter," she says. When they get out he right away puts his arm inside hers. Together like that they look at me. Both smile. He waves as I pull away. What's this all about, I ask my dog once we're alone again. Walt's on his back, snorting and pulling and pushing himself along the length of the seat. He can't seem to get enough of whatever it is they left behind. "Walt, what is it for god sakes?" It's like he's answering me all right, but from some other country.

SEA LIONS

"Hey you pack of water dogs!" The racket they make I make
back, aawk, aawk, aawk, thinking I got the sound just about
right. Silence, or sea-lion laughs all around at the arm-waving
animal there on the beach without a tail, or language, who just
doesn't get it. They move off, a big male in the lead, his head, im-
mense back coming up out of the water before he disappears,
before they all do. What goes out of them across the water and
comes into me is what I want to know. This heart of mine, erratic
now, an old paddleball. If later I close my eyes I can see them
down there in the depth, their soft, dark bodies, huge eyes, mov-
ing in and out of this invisible rope they braid all the way to the
Queen Charlotte Islands. Years ago aboard ship on a dead calm
sea at night we came on a vast herd. Not moving. There was al-
most no noise except for our engines. What were they doing out
there going nowhere? You could see for a hundred miles, it was
that clear. Overhead, stars, millions of stars.

IT DEBATES NOTHING

Goes where it wants to, is never,
strictly speaking, regional. Docks,
even the good ones, it breaks up.
A man walking out on one
loaded down with fishing tackle,
food, his foul weather gear,
needs to be careful. He could fall in.
That always settles any argument
about who's in charge. Boats,
I think, water likes more.
Take the submarine, for example,
the friendly way it curves into water
like a seal, with so much integrity
it can go beneath the surface
of any argument wind wants to make.
Grebes, too, and soft-bellied ducks
have this smooth way of slipping below
when it suits them. I like water
mostly because, well, it teaches patience.
Say you're trapped inside
a compartment aboard a ship
that's going down. On top of the water,
below the water, does it really matter?
Why spend your last moments feeling bad.
It was always coming in.

JACKSCREW

What we didn't know
was how much we'd have to give in.
The way we could only throw flowers
to the place where the plane went in.
Nobody can imagine what the eighty-eight people felt,
saw, in those last moments.
"Please fasten your seat belts,"
the flight attendant probably said.

Our lives—all those plans—turn
on a jackscrew. The earth too.
6.5 on the Richter scale
makes that clear. You try to hold on
while the whole house lets go
of everything you've acquired.

Hello! Good-bye! The only thing
you may have time to say.
What turns us all around
to the sudden need for community.
People out their back doors
waving their arms to neighbors
they haven't talked to in years.

Chief Seattle, an old Taoist,
would not have been so surprised
at the indignation of crows
shaken from their perches
or to see the whole city lift up
across the water, then settle back down.

Getting the names of birds after fifty turns into some kind of
race. You still can't see the finish line—it's not that bad or good—
but now you know it's up there. So, when Gary slowed the lit-
tle pickup outside of Manchester to point out to me the greater
scaup with its stunning blue bill, water bubbling off as it pulled
up beach kelp, I was surprised. Even more at my immediate feel-
ings of, what can I say, envy, that he got there first and with so
much authority, the name, the way he already owned it. You
couldn't exactly see the flag he'd planted in that gorgeous bird's
back, but it was there all right. Maybe I got even, if that doesn't
sound too tit for tat, when I introduced him to my humble little
pied-billed grebe in its winter plumage on a walk by Tulalip Bay.
I babbled on a bit and being less than gracious I think I imme-
diately repeated the name, like I was Shackleton discovering the
South Pole. What gets into us after fifty that has us slowing down
at the same time we're speeding up? Birds pick it up. We're not
coming with a gun and they know it. That each one has a name
and we're out to learn it, well, that's a human thing. There's al-
ways going to be the urgency toward the end and we've got a lot
of birds to go.

THE LATE HOUR

It's a pleasure sometimes
to notice my aging hands
holding each other,
so familiar,
the fingers interlocked.

Evenings I allow myself
two really good poems
to read over and over,
my warm milk and crackers
I suppose.

Over my shoulder
the radio turned low
brings in the same old song
every night: love me
somebody, please!

My own loneliness
when it's good
I can tell you is so vast
nothing will satisfy it
but the late hour
and a sky full of stars.

I was some kind of car
backing out of my body.
It was amusing though, watching
me standing there
staring at something at my feet,
I think now the serpentine stone,
blazing in the water, I picked up
and put in my pocket, which struck me
as funny from behind, like this person
who really looks his age,
stands with a limp, potbellied,
thinks there's something
to hold on to. Pretty stones
at the bottom of consciousness
litter the beaches here,
so dense in thought
they're good for picking up,
feeling, turning over in the hand
before dropped again
or heaved back out into the surf.
This is a human activity—
all over the world
wherever stones wash up
somebody will be standing there
holding one,
looking more than anything, lost.
Nobody knows why.

ALL THE SIGNS ARE HERE

It's not all that mysterious
really, the new crop of brown spots
on both forearms.
Three fingers on my left hand
gone dead white from old nerve damage,
and my dog coming out
from under the covers
seven-times-ten or seventy years
old with breath to kill.
So, all the signs are here,
we're leaving. Happy days.
Good-bye to receding gums,
the waste of despair,
old loves chewed on
way too long.
Clouds that make themselves up
over and over
as if change is all that's permanent.
There's nothing sad here.
Think of that little red double-ender,
its paint chipped, fading,
going out and coming in.

DRUMS

Rain on the roof, the intermittent wind, and the sound of drums from the longhouse at the end of the bay. Walt lets out a long, low sound, not a growl, different from anything I've heard out of him before. These drums and deep, gruff chant of human voices coming across the water create a chorus he wants to join. I reach down to pat him on the rump, keep time with the beat. I don't romanticize. I've seen the piles of hocked turquoise rings, bracelets, watchbands, mostly for booze, the junkyard existence of reservation life in the Southwest. The signs here too on the way into the Indian settlement: Drug Free Neighborhood. Recovering the village is hard work. "Relax, Walt," I say, running my hand down his back. But he is relaxed. It's me who's edgy. Pretty soon my breathing eases. I feel the warmth of the cotton sheets. Maybe I'm already asleep when they enter my mind, the large flock of sanderlings we watched earlier on the spit, skittish, landing and taking off all together, tiny, dark winged, and then swirling and veering over our heads, sun lighting their snowy underbellies like someone suddenly pulling a Venetian blind. The sweet thud of so many wings.

FOUND POEM

All circumstantial
what washes up on the beach,
the lady's cowboy belt,
medium, "Love Tanned" leather
it says on the back. Nordstrom,
evidence of what, a storm at sea?
Unlikely. No crime in abandonment
though. Excessive wear
on the last hole suggests a small waist.
Imagine a good time out there,
one of those summer boats
that sometimes cruise Tulalip Bay
watching sea lions
tie themselves in soft knots
the way they do
(churning the water so much,
excited seagulls swoop down
hoping for fish)
might make a woman feel
like she had too much on.
What we have to go on though:
no mischief reported
or thief, warm weather,
the solid silver buckle,
probably Mexican, charming,
but not handmade.

DECEMBER

tide
hangs up
over
a red log
a long
twisted
yellow sock
of skin
pulled inside
out
by a jaw
full of seesaw
teeth
and two eye
holes
below which
hang
a white train
of salmon
bones,
MERRY
CHRISTMAS

A BEACH THAT WON'T BE RUSHED

We have no patience for tides,
their ups and downs
move too slow for us.
It's as much as anything
the gait that takes us
down the beach
faster than driftwood
floats in. Or waves—
there are just too many
to take in, or the birds
that ride them.
It's a human problem: the grebe
won't stay put, or the loon
long enough, or they do
and we're already past them
walking toward what's up ahead.
We come home still restless
with sand in our shoes,
worn out by the slowness,
the utter slowness of a beach
that won't be rushed.

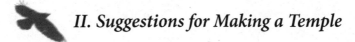 *II. Suggestions for Making a Temple*

SUGGESTIONS FOR MAKING A TEMPLE

Keep it small. One door is the rule, so you have to come out
the same one you go in. That's important. And no windows.
When I say small I mean something you can get your finger in
so that it's just between you and the clay. One day, for example,
when I pulled my trimming tool back out the clay folded over the
steel to form a soft ridge around the opening. So beautiful, right
there I knew I'd want to keep on, if I could, making that sweet,
little door. I coil-build my temples so they're mostly irregular.
From the outside the walls always belly out before they curve
back in. Also, and this is important, I paddle my temples. They're
small enough to hold in one hand and rotate while I strike them
with the other. If I've done it right the walls flex as they grow
stronger. The tool doesn't matter. I use a surveyor's stake I found
one day on a walk through a construction site, fir maybe, lots of
deep grains that leave a leafy pattern. Remember, in making your
temple the only light inside is what comes through your door.
Also, watch how you attach the roof. Birds somehow still get into
mine. People tell me my temples are special, that I've broken new
ground. That's unlikely. What's older than a temple? Hope is re-
quired though. And you have to be thankful, as dark as it is in
there, for what you've made. Nothing's more forgiving than clay.
If you don't like your temple, well, make another one.

FEELING UP THE WORLD

We have ten ways
of feeling up the world.
The rest is about courage
and you have to figure
to wake up is always good luck,
daylight being the first seduction.
Then it's on to the oatmeal
or whatever it is you eat
to stay alive
and that's what we're talking about,
not about the job,
the big truck you drive
on icy roads. It doesn't mean
ten gloved fingers
wrapped around a steering wheel,
or getting in a third load
before dark.

God bless the little dead man
who rides on my shoulder,
my constant companion—
a Buddhist joke—
who likes to niggle me.

Empty your bowl.
Don't complain.
Where the road curves
and falls away
into you don't know what,
take it.

DOGS THAT BARK

Figure about every third house in America
there's a dog. Walk down any street
at six in the morning, Portland, Oregon,
Chicago, it doesn't matter,
a dog will announce your arrival.
All the dogless neighbors will hate the barking
but what can they do about it, really,
stand back from the window and fume:
"That son-of-a-bitch had better shut that dog up
or I'm gonna shoot both of them," he'll say.
It's male talk. Harkens back to when a man
could go for his gun to bring the world right.
His wife, rolling her eyes, will tell him to come back
to the table, have some more coffee.
Up and down the streets of our country
it's like this inside the houses. Men
going for their guns and women restoring order—
"Harry, stop your huffing, you're not goin' to do anything
of the kind." Meanwhile, outside
the chorus of dogs continues: Gus,
the German Shepherd on Maple,
throws the bone of his song to Jake,
the black mutt on 37th who rouses
scruffy Vinnie over on Bybee to join in.
It's a grudging peace in our country
but dogs, like it or not, build neighborhood.

HARVEST

for Gary

Fifty miles inside Washington, alongside
some now-famous bay with a new name,
we pull to a stop, me behind my old friend
where he, archival in these matters,
tells me about the Bruce brothers, who in 1853
made a killing by harvesting the oysters
here and shipping them all to San Francisco.
It's a brief stop, coming as it does
between wind and heavy rain.
Then off again, his black tailgate
I follow, somehow comforting, taking us home.

Who is this man, I start to wonder, up ahead,
whose little truck sways to the wash
of the oncoming logging trucks,
whose life years ago weaved inextricably into mine?
And why do I feel a little stab of urgency
now when traffic or curving road
or blinding rain separates us for a time
from each other? We've been so long
following the same map I suppose,
the poems we write, our shared wonder, grief,
I put off thinking about up ahead
to five miles past the rest stop
at such and such a junction he's already
pointed out to me, where he'll have to turn off.

Yes, I know what's coming for us all,
the signs we have to follow
where I fly by him, honking, waving,
the blur of rain,
watching in my rearview mirror
as long as I can his little truck slow,
yellow signal light blinking, then turn
and disappear.

THE GIFT

Einstein, an inner-directed man,
had no trouble explaining why his schnapps
didn't float up off the table.
Gravity was a knot, he said, God tied our galaxy in,
forever, or if you like, energy bound up
in an eternal state of push and pull
and that's what keeps our shoes
beside the bed at night,
our dreams mostly ordinary.
It's only the child who points
to the invisible wind with delight,
squishes his banana into his ear
and expects it to talk. What's given,
and that's surely everything, some call grace.
I like that. It's like I'm this marvelous gift
to myself I get to keep unwrapping.

GOING PUBLIC

"Sometimes I think I too should go public, put it all
out there, as it were, the whole, sad portfolio."

In the dream I wake up chauffeured
in a blue Lincoln, my laptop flashing
up-to-the-minute quotes from my broker.
Awake again, my knees both ache
and I fall back into our little group
where the only market share is the good poem
that hasn't been written yet.
Don't laugh. It takes all kinds,
my father used to say. He was a failure too
except when he pulled his hickory-
handled saw across a 2 x 6
then flowed back into the wood
like they needed each other,
the cut straight and true.
This was before the Skil saw
and *Nightly Business Report*—
Paul Kangas in his gray, bulging suit,
telling us who the winners and losers are.
Don't get me wrong, I'd own stock too
but a job was out of the question
after the first real poem came along.
Insider trading I take to mean
planting ahead, the winter crop:
climbing squash for sure
and those big-shouldered leeks
the garden looks up to.
Years ago my mentor said to me,

"Tom, whatever happens to you
in life, you'll always have the poetry."
I've tried, over the years—one wife dead,
another gone—to hold on to whatever this gift is
that keeps me poor.

WHAT FIRE DOES TO CLAY

Grief.
No place you want to hang around,
you might think.
No different than fall light
though, boring through low clouds
to make a red sky
you can't turn away from.
What fire does to clay.
Give it a chance goes the advice
about what comes out of the kiln.
My sculpture turned black
from the ash, the heat so intense
it collapsed both eyes
and melted an ear down
to a golden lump.
Gifts of the fire for sure.
When Gretel died
I thought I would too,
thinking there was no limit
to how much a person could be stretched.
Silly me. It's the intensity of love.
Grieve, if anything, its loss,
the curve flat, feelings ordinary.

THE ENTHUSIAST

Mine was a coarse intelligence,
I knew that, a man
upon whom nuance was wasted.
Clay in my hands
did not refine itself
into anything more than a dog head
that could also be a pig head—
you could choose—vessels
good for nothing, my pinch pots
closed off to meaning
or the thick, squat stupas
I'd made, devotional, the way I imagined
a hunkered down Buddha.
In the end my heart
still banging out those small notes
I could not hear.
An enthusiast, that's what I was,
big knuckled, splitter of wood,
guffawer of the dumb joke,
enchanted always by the obvious—
birds, yes especially birds,
the pigeon-toed crow,
clumsy in its deportment,
who had no particular song
but who did not want to be anything else.

THROUGH A DOG'S EYES

What do I know about what he sees
when he looks at me, my dog.
If eyes say anything, though,
I'm twice as nice as I allow myself to think I am.
He puts me in league with the special things
of the world like the Guggenheim
or the new bridge over the Willamette
that you have to imagine being built.
Really a people-friendly bridge,
which means noisy cars (no trucks allowed)
take the lower span, but the upper one
where the sun shines all day
is just for people and you can see for miles,
Mt. Hood right in front of you and every day
a different country's flag up there
flapping in the wind. That's how my dog
wants me to see me. For sure
there is something coming out of him
and going into me which is what a bridge does
between two shores, allows ideas across
and vegetables and fruit and other people's dogs.
When you're a bridge the world just naturally comes
to you is what I think he wants me to think of me.

TO MAKE AN OWL MAKE A POEM

No tools required.
Not so hard if you start small,
say with the beak
which is entirely manageable,
pinching a little ball of soft stoneware
between the tool of your thumb
and index finger—
the head begins to sprout
from the spontaneous eyes
the tips of the fingers just naturally make
so you see immediately
where the broad shoulders
want to begin.

To make an owl
is to forget yourself,
the coins in your pockets,
failed love,
the fame you'll never have.

To make an owl make a poem
you have to
be very nearly out of control
in the squish and push
and pull of it,
to make a poem
stand up
solitary
for you like that
and be an owl.

BULL PINE

The last woman I kissed
I kissed all night and that's a lot of trees.
If one's good why are two better,
the multiplication of trunks?
Is it the intensity of the gaze,
the looking in
that causes bull pine to turn lover?
How does logic go,
her black hair falling down
onto my face, the expert way
she removes my socks
with her toes—what better explains
what wind does to trees—
I can hardly bear, alone,
the sound of pine needles
waking me when they hit the roof
of my little trailer at night.

SUGAR LIFT

It's not sadness, exactly
(that there is no sun
or fleet of clouds overhead,
just an old, paint-spattered ladder
leaning against the house
in front of which stands a little man
in overalls
with a bucket in one hand,
brush in the other,
and behind him his black dog,
both leaning back, looking up
at the work,
the earth underneath their six feet
carrying them along
from one paint job to the next)
but something.

THIS TREE

1.

This tree, a breed too
(there are, after all,
so many in the city)
steps out onto West 90th,
groomed by light,
her spread limbs
sap rising
then falling
in a black hat,
a breezy god
lifting the hair,
leaf, saddle.

2.

Rothko would agree,
horse is a feeling
about color.
Tree too.
And if it's not about God,
forget it.
Now, *you* paint them in.

3.

What's good about art?
What the legs can't get around,
imagination will.

4.

Oh life, beauty *is,*
getting your hands in it,
braiding the tail
of the chestnut.

CELLO

1.

My friend likes to say, "Of course, you're a poet."
This always in response to my difficulties.
Then he smiles. He's right.
To eat to stay alive isn't good enough.
An old lesson in aesthetics: the chicken wings have to hurt
you too or who cares.

2.

Joy, when it lasts, is always a dark licorice. Look!
The Chrysler Building at night. Topped off
in silver scallops. Beautiful. Yes, OK,
but there's nothing there to make us sweat
under the covers.

3.

Geese on water, what a pretty sight.
But it won't last, no. It's the one with the broken wing
pushing itself in a circle, the despair of its mate.
The end of hope is what we learn by heart.

4.

What's sad is what we've come for.
The bare, lighted stage.
Four strings and a wooden box
where one note can turn over in us the deepest soil.

STUMP TOWN

This time three nudes
at Stump Town Barista
coming up out of the copper plate,
Tom's "paper," while he sips his caffè latte
talking over his right hand
doodling its way
toward original sin.
But that doesn't stop him
from scratching them in anyway,
mixing up the anatomy, their intentions.
It's what can happen in a free society
when you unbutton the mind
to what's around you in the room:
A woman in short shorts and yellow blouse
who can't keep her legs still
under the table. A hairy
blond dog lying in the doorway,
in the sunlight,
halfway out, halfway in,
leaning toward what we can't smell.
All the parts interchangeable
his nudes say, the head of steam
boiling the white milk
that's eased into the espresso—
on the floor a big sack
of beans from Bolivia.

RICH'S LETTER

I know what I must look like right now
standing in front of Morrison Books
on 12th and Hoyt, unemployed, no hat on, rain dripping
off my chin, the back of my head, but I don't mind
I gotta tell ya, discovering Rich's letter
Scotch-taped to the inside glass—
Her reasons in '97 for saying no to the presidential
invitation to read poetry at the White House.
It's just then it happens when I hear my own name called
from up the street, "Tom!" Portland tilts
to the right and all the water puddles
up and down 12th begin to shimmer, the one
right in front of me shakes itself like an old dog.
A woman under a tattered umbrella
looks at me like she knows right now
I'm being singled out because
a block away my friend's ordinary arm,
at the end of which wave five pickle-shaped
fingers, sends goose bumps through me.
It's that moment when good and evil can't enter
but light or a flock of white pigeons,
resident birds from the Morrison Bridge, can
or the Mack truck right in front of me,
idling, its huge tires, chrome rims, dripping rainwater.

REDWING

He's inside my mouth,
no, beside the road
clinging to a May cattail.
It gets confusing, what's in,
what's out, like saying the sun's up
or down when we know it's none of those
and words, even the good ones
can only pepper the edge
of feelings and that's what we're after
here which means going down
the throat to get to where he lives.
But if I start smiling because
there's a bird inside me
you can guess how long I'd be allowed
out, alone. So, like a few others,
to remain free I sort of play that down
when pointing to a world
that's not supposed to be
which only means
they've been piling rocks on me
for years—an old Puritan trick—to get me
to come around to their god.
I must be Buddhist. The bell
has its own words for it—water, wind,
the quiet world a bird brings.

ALL THAT'S REAL

This house won't last.
It's like the potter's bowl,
dreamy in its green glaze
but already cracks forming
what's certain.

Last night, snow, good old snow,
it banged on all the windows,
leaned into the house.

All that's real,
memory, wind,
what's here and not here,
my dead father
with nowhere else to go
comes through the front door
in a white cloud
stomping his boots.

Right now I'm smoking
a dark La Gloria Cubana.
It's such a pleasure to be here,
to smoke it,
to smoke it into ashes.

TRAILER SONG

The cupboard so small no room
for Walls economy size raspberry
jam, except on the counter
against my Hamilton Beach toaster, nice, though,
everything sort of arm in arm in here,
the port-a-potty deodorant
next to *Field Guild to North American Birds*
leaning into the *Bhagavad Gita* held up
only by the weight of the rotund sculpture,
my little nude. Made her myself. Not for sale.
One works hard to get a life so small
where just breathing sways the pans,
knives hanging over the sink,
the hand towel half-hiding Meher Baba
above the little three-burner stove.
Any move in here has to be thought out,
deliberate, not to kick over the dog bowl,
untangle my one leg the table has room for.
No contraries either. One wool slipper
gone off somewhere. The other paired
with my Hi-Tec boot. You want grief,
sorry, at my age it's a waste of space
though a hard wind, when it comes,
tries to frighten me, pulling at the roof vent
with its metal pliers, the jacked-up tire
that keeps the jam from sliding, the books level.
It's a minimalist life. What's outside
is almost in—the beautiful flicker, self-contained,
can go anywhere, startled me when it landed
on the roof this morning, its nails scratching
the metal. If I fall, well, I'm bound to catch the bed
or God's call, if He should, on the first ring.

GLOSSARY

1. Chengdu: the capitol of Sichuan Province.

2. Chongqing: a city in Sichuan Province and capitol of Nationalist China during the Sino-Japanese War.

3. Ciqikou: an ancient Chinese settlement on the banks of the Jialing River in Chongqing.

4. Dharma: the cosmic law of Buddhism and its dutiful observance—right conduct.

5. Dufu: famous Tang poet.

6. Ehru: an eighth century, two-string, lute-form instrument.

7. Han: the country of China, also meaning "long suffering."

8. I Ching: The Book of Change.

9. Jie fang bei: an open market in Shapingba.

10. Lao wai: foreigner.

11. Lieschimu: Tomb of the Martyrs, also the historical location of the Nationalist prison camp where hundreds of Communists were executed.

12. Manchu: Manchu Dynasty, 1643–1912.

13. Nanchong: a city in Sichuan Province, China.

14. Shapingba: suburb of Chongqing.

15. Shi ba ti: twenty-one steps.

16. Yuan fen: fate, but more precisely, the Buddhist belief that we find ourselves where we are supposed to be in the world, and often with old friends.

ACKNOWLEDGMENTS

There are many people to thank in the writing of *Wu Wei*. Help has come in all sorts of ways, mostly though through their enthusiasm and suggestions, many of which not only nudged me toward revision and better poems but inspired new ones. Suffice it is to say, it's a family enterprise, making poems. Thank you all: Mary Judge, Gary Thompson, Quinton Duval, Dennis Schmitz, Chip Blake, David Duncan, Kris Wood, Ed Field, John Bateman, Sandra Loy, David Nichols, T.J. Christenson, Yun Deuk, Tony Petrosky, Ellen Bishop, Sarah Phelan, George Manner, Margaret Eissler, Carol Haight, Jenny Case, Aston Case, Len Hudson, Tom Kearcher, and Walt, my dog.

Acknowledgment is made to the editors of the following publications in which some of these poems first appeared:

China Dancing, Cedar House Books, Seattle.

Willow Springs Press, University of Eastern Washington: "Wu Wei," "The Enthusiast," "Through A Dog's Eyes."

And We the Creatures, Dream Horse Press, Felton, California: "Dogs That Bark."

Orion: "The Names of Birds."

Cutbank, University of Montana: "Bull Pine."

The Tom Project, A Collaboration of Three Portland, Oregon, Artists: "Sugar Lift," "Charming Phenomenal World."

Hubbub Magazine: "Harvest."

Camus Review, University of Montana: "Trailer Song."

TOM CRAWFORD's four previous collections of poems include *If It Weren't for Trees, Lauds,* which won the Oregon Book Award, *China Dancing,* and *The Temple on Monday,* winner of the ForeWord Book of the Year Award. He has been recipient of fellowships from the Oregon Arts Commission and the National Endowment for the Arts and his work has been widely published in journals and anthologies. He has lectured and taught at colleges and universities throughout the western United States, taught two years in the People's Republic of China, and six years as a professor of English at Chonnam National University, Kwangju, Korea. He lives in Santa Fe, New Mexico.

MORE POETRY FROM MILKWEED EDITIONS

To order books or for more information,
contact Milkweed at (800) 520-6455
or visit our Web site (www.milkweed.org).

Blue Lash
JAMES ARMSTONG

Turning Over the Earth
RALPH BLACK

Morning Earth:
 Field Notes in Poetry
JOHN CADDY

The Phoenix Gone,
 The Terrace Empty
MARILYN CHIN

The Art of Writing:
 Lu Chi's Wen Fu
TRANSLATED FROM THE
 CHINESE BY SAM HAMILL

The Porcelain Apes of
 Moses Mendelssohn
JEAN NORDHAUS

Playing the Black Piano
BILL HOLM

Good Heart
DEBORAH KEENAN

Furia
ORLANDO RICARDO MENES

Firekeeper:
 Selected Poems
PATTIANN ROGERS

Some Church
DAVID ROMTVEDT

For My Father, Falling Asleep
 at Saint Mary's Hospital
DENNIS SAMPSON

Atlas
KATRINA VANDENBERG

MILKWEED EDITIONS

Founded in 1979, Milkweed Editions is the largest independent, nonprofit literary publisher in the United States. Milkweed publishes with the intention of making a humane impact on society, in the belief that good writing can transform the human heart and spirit. Within this mission, Milkweed publishes in five areas: fiction, nonfiction, poetry, children's literature for middle-grade readers, and the World As Home—books about our relationship with the natural world.

JOIN US

Milkweed depends on the generosity of foundations and individuals like you, in addition to the sales of its books. In an increasingly consolidated and bottom-line-driven publishing world, your support allows us to select and publish books on the basis of their literary quality and the depth of their message. Please visit our Web site (www.milkweed.org) or contact us at (800) 520-6455 to learn more about our donor program.

Interior design by Rachel Holscher
Typeset in 10.5/15 Minion Pro
by Prism Publishing Center
Printed on acid-free Rolland Enviro 100 paper
by Friesens Corporation.